African Politics in Comparative Perspective

This book reviews fifty years of research on politics in Africa. It synthe-
sizes insights from different scholarly approaches and offers an origi-
nal interpretation of the knowledge accumulated over the years. It dis-
cusses how research on African politics relates to the study of politics
in other regions and mainstream theories in comparative politics. It
focuses on such key issues as the legacy of a movement approach to
political change, the nature of the state, the economy of affection, the
policy deficit, the agrarian question, gender and politics, and ethnicity
and conflict. It concludes by reviewing what scholars agree upon and
what the accumulated knowledge offers as insights for more effective
political and policy reforms. This book is an ideal text in undergrad-
uate and graduate courses in African and comparative politics as well
as in development-oriented courses in political science and related dis-
ciplines. It is also of great relevance to governance and development
analysts and to practitioners in international organizations.

Goran Hyden is distinguished professor in political science at the
University of Florida. His publications include *Beyond Ujamaa in
Tanzania* (1980); *No Shortcuts to Progress* (1983); *Governance and
Politics in Africa*, coedited with Michael Bratton (1992); and *Making
Sense of Governance*, coauthored with Julius Court and Kenneth Mease
(2004). He served as president of the African Studies Association in
1995. He has also served as a consultant on African development to
many international agencies.